Bargil Pixner/George Hintlian
A. van der Heyden

The glory
of Bethlehem

I. Sheep tended by Arab shepherds in the fields of Bethlehem — a scene practically unchanged since biblical times.

The glory of Bethlehem

Judson Press Edition 1986
Judson Press, Valley Forge, PA

Printed in Belgium by Offset Printing Van Den Bossche

Design: FRITS VESTERS
Production Consultant: BOB VARI
Editorial Assistant: Georgette Corcos

*II. Bethlehem women still wear today the same head-dress
they have been wearing since the time of the Crusades.*
III. Sunrise over Bethlehem.

ISBN — 0-8170-1109-9

Contents

Introduction

1. Road sign near Bethlehem.

Bethlehem, the town which this book brings you in pictures and text, is only the tangible form of a dream, a vision which Mankind has treasured for almost two thousand years. Every year at Christmas time there is a little Bethlehem in every church and in many homes throughout the Christian world. There, in miniature, are re-created the manger ("because there was no room for them in the inn"), the shepherds and the humble beasts, and the Holy Family under the star of Bethlehem.

When you visit Bethlehem today you will see a small town, quite unlike other famous holy cities in the world, and remarkably unchanged since the time of Christ. However, although it seems to be a town of the past, Bethlehem has developed with the times; the arts and crafts are encouraged and modern improvements have been introduced for the well-being of its inhabitants without spoiling its quaint character. The fruit, the bread, the water, the scents in the air, even the dress of the local peasants, are much the same as they were in biblical times.

In the centre of the town stands the ancient Church of the Nativity, where on Christmas Eve a midnight mass is celebrated. The pomp of the world comes to Bethlehem and touches it briefly, and nowadays the event is carried by television broadcast to all corners of the earth. Then the little town returns to its age-old quietness and holy peace.

But Bethlehem has known many upheavals and troubles since the days when King David, one thousand years before Christ, longed for a drink of water from the well at the gate of his natal city. It was conquered and reconquered many times, and suffered at the hands of ruthless men. Nevertheless, history has dealt not unkindly with Bethlehem, and on the whole it has survived well the passage of the centuries and the ambitions of rulers.

You see before you a unique place adored by hundreds of millions, its very name imbued with holiness. It is nevertheless a living town, a natural part of the land, the sacred and the mundane blending in it harmoniously. Yet, although people conduct their everyday life in and about Bethlehem as if it were not one of the most famous spots on earth, the very atmosphere breathes a kind of serenity you will never forget.

Welcome to Bethlehem!

Elias Freij
Mayor of Bethlehem

"And Joseph also went up from Galilee, out of the city of Nazareth, into Judaea, unto the city of David, which is called Bethlehem; because he was of the house and lineage of David; to be taxed with Mary his espoused wife, being great with child" (Luke 2:4).

In those days Nazareth was a mere hamlet cradled in the foothills of Galilee, unknown to either the Bible or history. For many generations it had been the residence of descendants of the House of David. They called themselves Natzoreans, after the words of the prophet Isaiah (11:1): "And there shall come forth a shoot out of the stock of Jesse, and a twig (*netzer*) shall grow forth out of his roots". It was after this *netzer* that the village of Nazareth was apparently called. According to the author Julius Africanus of Emmaus, these descendants of David lived in villages bearing Messianic names such as Nazara (Village of the Twig) and Kokhaba (Village of the Star). A village of the latter name existed north of Nazareth, and a second one in the Bashan region a short walking distance from Bethsaida. There, according to Africanus, the Davidic family kept the genealogical records used to prove its royal descent. In this way the Natzoreans lived in the pious expectation that one day the Anointed of Israel, the Messiah, would arise from their midst. They liked to apply the words of the prophet

2. Like this Arab farmer, Joseph loaded his belongings on a donkey when he moved to Bethlehem.

2

3

3. Caesar Octavius Augustus.
4. Present-day Nazareth bears little re-semblance to the hamlet of Jesus' days.

in respect to themselves: "Thy people also shall be all righteous (*zaddikim*), they shall inherit the land for ever; the branch (*netzer*) of My planting, the work of My hands, wherein I glory", and "The spirit of the Lord God is upon me; because the Lord has anointed me to bring good tidings to the humble..." (Isaiah 60:21; 61:1). Jesus too quoted this text from Isaiah when preaching in the synagogue in his native town. He, however, gave a vastly different interpretation from the one the status-conscious Natzoreans would have liked. Jesus refused to restrict the benefits of his wondrous powers to his ambitious kinsmen, with the result that they drove him out of the town (see Luke 4:16-30).

Joseph the carpenter and his betrothed wife Mary were also Natzoreans. Through God's miraculous intervention Mary had become pregnant, and both knew that the soon-to-be-born child would be the Messiah of Israel. But they kept the secret to themselves. From the ancient prophecy of Micah they also knew that the Messiah would not be born in Galilee, but in Bethlehem. So they decided to move there. A contributory reason for their decision was the census ordered by Emperor Augustus, who wanted

4

5. The Herodian Temple wall, at which pious Jews pray today, already existed when Joseph and Mary brought their child to the Temple.

6. The Citadel of Jerusalem, formerly Herod's main palace, in winter dress. The base of Phasael's Tower has withstood time.

5

6

THE JOURNEY TO BETHLEHEM

7

7. First view of Bethlehem from the direction of Mar Elias Monastery.

to streamline his revenue-collection system. Under normal circumstances this would not have caused Joseph to subject his heavily-pregnant wife to the stresses of such a long and arduous journey. The evangelist Luke, however, stresses this fact in order to firmly associate the incarnation of the Son of God with the great historical figures of his time.

After fierce internal struggles Emperor Augustus had achieved the peak of his power. He was the architect of the *Pax Romana*, which for some years had re-established peace and security in his domain. In Jerusalem Herod was his crafty but devoted vassal, but the people hated this judaized

8. Bir el-Kadismu (Well of the Repose) on the road to Bethlehem, where Mary is said to have rested. Construction of the modern water conduit necessitated the closure of the mouth of the well.

9

9. *The ruins of the once famous Kathisma Monastery (Mary's resting place) near Mar Elias. It was associated with the appearance of the star that guided the Magi (Matthew 2:9).*

Idumaean, who in the year 37 B.C. had finally defeated Antigonus, the last king of the Hasmonaean priestly dynasty. Herod the Great was a much-feared tyrant, personally courageous but cruel and intensely jealous. Whenever he considered his throne to be endangered, his reaction was swift and utterly ruthless — even if it involved his own immediate family. The first to fall victim was the High Priest Aristobulus, brother of his "adored" wife Mariamne. The next to die was their mother, and finally Mariamne herself and the two children she had borne him. Herod's murdering of the children of Bethlehem was considered a minor incident, not worthy of historical mention. Yet this cruel ruler was one of the greatest builders of antiquity, his greatest achievement being the Temple in Jerusalem. His predecessors had left him two palaces: Baris, a fortress situated in the north-western corner of the Temple esplanade, became the imposing Antonia;

10. *View of the hills of Bethlehem beyond the cupola of Mar Elias Monastery.*

10

the Hasmonaean palace was extended and embellished with wall paintings and mosaics. In the latter Jesus was to stand trial before Pilate. In 23 B.C. Herod built another sumptuous palace in the north-western corner of the city for himself and his numerous wives and children. Here he received an endless stream of guests from all the corners of the world. Here, too, he was visited by the Magi from the East who, guided by the star, had set out to find the new-born King of the Jews.

Joseph and Mary passed the palace on their way to Bethlehem through Jerusalem. Mary would have glanced meekly at the imposing edifice. Did she guess the dangers which threatened from the powerful man behind these forbidding walls? The two lone wanderers passed Beth-Hakerem, the site of the present kibbutz Ramat Rahel. Tradition has it that just before reaching the ridge near the present monastery of Mar Elias they rested at a still-existing well, the Bir el-Kadismu (Well of the Repose). According to a legend, Mary had a vision here of two peoples: one rejoicing in the birth of the Messiah, the other refusing to accept him.

Upon reaching the ridge the view of the small town opened up before them. This was Bethlehem Ephratah, their ancestral home. To the east the craggy slopes of the Judaean Mountains descended steeply to the Dead Sea; on the horizon the Mountains of Moab glowed purple in the rays of the

11. Bethlehem borders on the Judaean Desert. In the background, beyond the Dead Sea, the Mountains of Moab, the ancestral territory of Ruth.
12. Harvesting methods in the fields of Bethlehem have changed little since the days of Ruth. In the background Herodium, Herod's "pyramid", where he wished to be buried.

13. *King David, founder of the Messianic Davidic line, made Bethlehem famous for all time.*

setting sun. In those far-off mountain regions their ancestor Ruth was born. Would they have been reminded of the opening words of the Book of Ruth: "And it came to pass in the days when the judges judged, that there was a famine in the land. And a certain man of Bethlehem in Judah went to sojourn in the field of Moab". Then follows the story of the two widows, the old and the young, the returning native and the stranger, who came to glean in the fields of Boaz, the Bethlehemite "in the beginning of the barley harvest". Boaz fell in love with Ruth and she bore him a son named Obed.

"Obed became the father of Jesse, who was the father of David". With these concluding words of the Book of Ruth the man is introduced through whom Bethlehem would become world famous: David, the shepherd, king of Israel, root of the Messianic branch. When God became disappointed with King Saul, he sent the prophet Samuel to Bethlehem to select the future king of Israel from among the eight sons of Jesse. After the seven oldest boys had passed before him, Samuel requested to see the youngest who was tending the sheep in the fields. This is how the Bible describes him: "Now he was ruddy, and withal of beautiful eyes, and goodly to look upon. And the Lord said: 'Arise, anoint him; for this is he'. Then Samuel took the horn of oil, and anointed him in the midst of his brethren; and the spirit of the Lord came mightily upon David from that day forward" (I Samuel 16:12-13).

Such thoughts might have come to Mary and Joseph's mind when they descended the heights of Mar Elias. Continuing their journey, they would have passed Rachel's Tomb. On his way to Bethlehem Ephratah, Jacob had buried his wife Rachel who died giving birth to their son Benjamin.

At last, Joseph and Mary entered the town. First of all they had to find lodgings for the night, for the baby was about to be born. But "there was no room for them in the inn" (Luke 2:7). Was it because they were too poor, or was there no suitably quiet place for Mary to bear her child? Being familiar with the place, Joseph remembered a shepherds' cave just outside the town. There he took Mary, and there, that same night, Jesus Christ was born.

14. *Rachel's Tomb along the road to Bethlehem Ephratah.*
15. *The Hebrew inscription on the cenotaph records the words of Jeremiah, as quoted in Matthew 2:18: "A voice is heard in Ramah, lamentation, and bitter weeping. Rachel weeping for her children . . . because they are not".*

HOW JESUS' BIRTHPLACE CAME TO BE KNOWN

Was Jesus actually born in Bethlehem? Several scholars have recently tried to disprove this tradition by pointing out that none of the early New Testament sources, such as the Epistles of St. Paul or the Gospel of Mark, make any mention of Bethlehem. This of course means very little, as there are countless great historical figures whose place of birth is unknown. People become famous as a result of what they say or do in the course of their lives. So it is not surprising that the earliest gospels do not mention Jesus' birth in Bethlehem — even assuming the authors were aware of the fact. The Apostles knew only the adult Jesus, and they spoke of what they had themselves seen or heard, beginning with the preachings of the Baptist, until Jesus' crucifixion and subsequent resurrection. This is the framework within which Mark, the author of the earliest gospel, places the life of Jesus, and so does John. We have no information that Jesus ever returned to Bethlehem. What his disciples would have known, however, was his descent from the House of David. The earliest indication of this comes from Paul himself, who in his letter to the Romans simply states, "Concerning his Son Jesus Christ our Lord, which was made of the seed of David according to the flesh..." (Romans 1:3).

Even so, knowledge of Jesus' birth in the town of David had for many years remained restricted to the *Dysposinoi* (the Lord's relatives), as the

16. Bethlehem means "Bread House". The proximity of the desert notwithstanding, the town has much fertile land. The fields supply grain, the olive groves oil and the vineyards grapes. "Ephratah", referring to the clan of the Ephratites, also means "the Fertile".

17

17. The city as seen towards the west.
18. View of the city towards the east.
The Mountains of Moab appear within
touching-distance.

members of his family were called. Recent scholars have shown that the composition of the early gospels is owed to certain historical events. Shortly after the death of Jesus' brother James in A.D. 62, a heresy was being propagated in Judaeo-Christian circles, according to which the "prophet" Jesus was adopted as God's son at the time of his baptism in the River Jordan. These same circles rejected the virgin birth, claiming that Jesus was the natural son of Joseph and Mary. This heresy would later be known as "Ebionism". Matthew and Luke's versions of the Gospel, written around the years A.D. 75-80, were attempts at countering this heretical current by emphasizing the apostolic doctrine of the pre-existence of the Son of God. As proof both of them — but independently of one another — told the story of his conception and birth.

Matthew might have received his information from existing relatives in the Nazarene village of Kokhaba (Village of the Star) in southern Syria. There stories — *haggadot* — circulated about Magi from the East who had followed a star which had guided them to the newly-born King of the Jews in Bethlehem. Luke, on the other hand, "having had perfect understanding of all things from the very first" (Luke 1:3), may have consulted close relatives such as Simeon Bar-Kleopha — Jesus' cousin and the second bishop of Jerusalem — for his source material about the early days of Jesus' life. Certain reminiscences of Mary were also handed down, perhaps as a written Aramaic *haggada*. This gives us two witnesses who, independent of each other, researched the issue and made known that Jesus was born in Bethlehem.

19

19. The place of the Manger.

20. Old road sign pointing to the Cave of the Nativity.
21. The site of the Church of the Nativity, where Emperor Hadrian planted a grove in honour of the pagan god Adonis.

Following the Edict of Milan (A.D. 312), Christianity emerged from its hiding place in the catacombs. At last Christians could openly identify with the sites they considered holy. In the year 326 the pious Empress Helena, mother of Constantine the Great, embarked on a pilgrimage to the Holy Land. Immediately after her arrival she instigated the construction of basilicas at the site of three "mystical grottoes" revered since the early days of Christianity. These were the grotto of Jesus' burial at Golgotha, the Cave of the Disciples (Eleona) on the Mount of Olives, and the Cave of the Nativity in Bethlehem. The question remains, however, whether the latter indeed marks the site of the manger in which Mary laid the infant Jesus. Could such a tradition have survived three centuries interspersed by numerous wars and persecutions? It is fortunate that few traditional sites in the Holy Land are so well documented as the Grotto of the Nativity in Bethlehem.

The first leader of the Christian community in Jerusalem was James, the "Lord's brother" (Galatians 1:19). He was succeeded by his cousin Simeon Bar-Kleopha, who was apparently crucified in around A.D. 100, at an advanced age, because of his Davidic descent and alleged Messianic pretensions. Jesus' mother, Mary, lived among the community until her death in about A.D. 50. The words, "But Mary kept all these things, and pondered them in her heart" (Luke 2:19), show that she reflected on the events which had taken place during Jesus' youth. We may assume that

20

21

22. *Tower adjoining the original entrance to the Cave of the Nativity.*
23. *The banner of the Greek-Orthodox.*

24. *The transept of the Church of the Nativity lies above the Grotto.*

25. In A.D. 135 Emperor Hadrian turned the Judaeo-Christian Nativity shrine into a pagan sanctuary.

26. "Now when Jesus was born in Bethlehem of Judaea in the days of Herod the king, behold there came wise men from the East to Jerusalem. . . . They saw the young child with Mary his mother, and fell down, and worshipped him" (Matthew 2:1, 11).

she used to visit nearby Bethlehem and the place of Jesus' birth. The various traditions were preserved among these early Jerusalem Christians. Already Justin Martyr, born in the year A.D. 100 in Neapolis (Nablus), knew of a grotto in Bethlehem in which Jesus had been born.

It is one of the ironies of history that the definite identification of many Jewish and Christian holy sites is owed to a pagan Roman emperor. Following the bloody repression of the Jewish Bar Kokhba insurrection (132-35), Emperor Hadrian reacted with the utmost severity to suppress any Jewish-inspired Messianic movement. The Jews were expelled from Jerusalem and all known Judaeo-Christian holy places were paganized, such as the Temple, the Siloam pool, the Bethesda pool, or Mamre, near Hebron. At the site of the Holy Sepulchre arose a temple of Venus and over the Grotto of the Nativity the Romans planted a grove dedicated to Adonis.

Origen, the foremost theologian of the 3rd century, appears to have visited this pagan cult place in the year 220, at which time he was also shown the place of Jesus' birth. He writes: "In Bethlehem the grotto was shown where, according to the Gospels, Jesus was born, as well as the manger in which, wrapped in swaddling clothes, he was lain. That what was shown to me is familiar to everyone in the area. The heathens themselves tell everyone who is willing to listen that in the said grotto a certain Jesus was born whom the Christians revered" (Contra Celsum I, 51).

Even the pagan cult of Adonis did not deter Christians from visiting the grotto. Around 315, ten years before the construction of the Basilica of the Nativity, Eusebius wrote: "Up till the present day the local population of Bethlehem bears witness to the ancestral tradition and proceeds to show visitors the grotto in which the Virgin gave birth to the Child". This means that Emperor Constantine could refer to a foundation in tradition and fact when in 326 he decided to found the Basilica of the Nativity on this spot.

27

28

28. *The Grotto of the Nativity.*

27. *The marble-faced trough in which Mary laid the child.*
29. *Many legends have been woven around the pointsettia, which flowers during the Christmas period. This one is from the Philippines.*

A CHRISTMAS LEGEND FROM THE PHILIPPINES

In addition to the countless beautiful flowers and plants, God created an unsightly shrub whose branches bore little more than coarse, green leaves and, at the end, small, seedy-looking knobs. The poor shrub was so ashamed that it grew only in inconspicuous and deserted locations.

One of these shrubs grew near the entrance of a cave situated near the little town of Bethlehem. One cold winter night a neglected-looking couple approached the cave from the road to Bethlehem. Mary and Joseph were exhausted from their long journey. The woman, hardly more than a girl, seemed desperate, for she was in labour and the baby could be born any time.

Joseph quickly entered the cave to make the necessary preparations for their stay. Mary remained standing in the dark night. Her hand brushed the plant with the coarse leaves. And behold, suddenly the leaves turned a brilliant red and the unsightly flower knobs turned bright with joy — for the Saviour was about to be born.

Since then it flowers every time it is Christmas on earth. ...People call it the "Christmas Flower".

29

30. *Modern sign to the Church of the Nativity.*

31. *Bethlehemites sunning themselves on remaining columns of the atrium of the Church of the Nativity.*

The present Church of the Nativity is one of the earliest Christian structures. The original basilica, erected in the 4th century by Constantine the Great, was enlarged and embellished by Emperor Justinian (527-65). In course of time the complex was expanded by the addition of several chapels and monasteries. On the south side churches and monasteries belonging to the Armenian and Greek Orthodox Churches adjoin the ancient basilica; at the northern end it is abutted by the Franciscan hospice and monastery and the Roman Catholic Church of St. Catherine.

About a quarter of the church's façade is covered by a fortress-like supporting wall which cradles the crumbling masonry as if to prevent it from falling down. The façade at one time was decorated with a colourful mosaic, which saved the church when, in the fateful year 614, almost all sanctuaries in the Holy Land were destroyed by the Persian invaders. How this happened is described in a letter from the Jerusalem Synod of the year 838:

"When the Persians, after having sacked all the towns in Syria, reached Bethlehem, they were greatly surprised to discover a representation of the Magi from Persia. Out of reverence and respect for their ancestors they decided to honour these sages by sparing the church. And this is how it has survived until this day".

When some two hundred years later the country was overrun by the Islamic Arabs, the fate of the church appeared once more in the balance. But their leader Omar decided that the place where their prophet Issa had been born out of the virgin Mariam deserved to be protected, and legend had it that he kneeled down in the southern apse of the church to pray to Mecca. The Mosque of Omar with its fine minaret which arises at the western

end of the church plaza commemorates this gesture of the prophet Moham-
med's immediate successor.

First impressions notwithstanding, the impregnable-looking church
façade is not without interest to the observant pilgrim. The original church
had three entrances, two of which have been bricked up. The central and
highest portal of Justinian's church was lowered during the Middle Ages;
the resulting pointed arch is still visible today. During the Ottoman era
this arch was reduced further, leaving the present low and narrow opening

32

32. Lintel of the main portal of Justinian's façade.

33. This pointed arch dates from Crusader times. During the Ottoman period it was partially walled up to prevent mounted horsemen from entering the church.

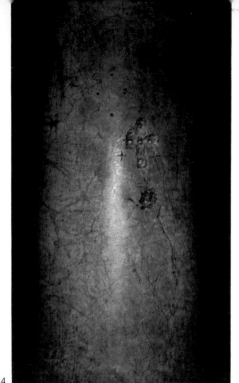

34

36

34. *One of the limestone columns.*
36. *Ray of light striking the choir of the Greek-Orthodox Church.*
37/38. *Brass lamps between the columns.*

37

35. *The late-Byzantine baptistry.*

35

38

which can only be passed when the visitor bends his head and knees. It is as if it wants to caution him: "Lower yourself, you proud one, if you want to approach God, who for your sake came to us as a child".

Immediately behind the entrance is a vestibule, the former narthex of Justinian's imposing church. The opposite door leads directly into the main body of the basilica. The interior, whose hallowed antiquity cannot but inspire the visitor with awe, is divided into a central nave and two side aisles. The stone for the numerous "golden-hued" supporting columns was quarried in Bethlehem, where Justinian's architects also made the pillars for Jerusalem's greatest church dedicated to Mary, the 'Nea'.

These limestone columns, which aroused the admiration of the Patriarch Sophronius, were during the Middle Ages painted with frescoes of the Apostles which unfortunately have faded almost completely. The clerestory windows below the elevated roof of the nave provide a bright illumination of the church interior. The remaining mosaics on the side walls and floor attest to the former splendour of this sanctuary. Since the removal of the decorated flat ceiling built by Justinian, the original pointed roof-structure from the days of Emperor Constantine is once more visible.

From the year 326 the empress-mother Helena zealously pursued the construction of the basilica at the site of the grotto. The place of the present sumptuous iconostasis (a decorated screen across the width of the sanctuary)

39. In about 635 Sophronius (later Patriarch) invokes the former splendour of the church: "How would I like to be in the small town of Bethlehem, where the Lord of All was born.
When entering the splendid four-fold hall, when the choir with the sublime three-fold apse of this holy mansion I would tread, how I would exult.
Beholding the many golden-hued columns and the finest ever achieved by mosaic-art, how would the clouds of care lift away.
I would gaze at the star-spangled ceiling overhead, for with the splendour of these labours the heavens are suffused.
May Christ grant me to see the beauty that is Bethlehem".

40

40. The reading of the Gospel.

originally contained an octagonal apsidial structure covering the grotto, into which the pilgrims could probably look through a large circular opening.

Apparently the original entrance to the grotto was from the main body of the church. Justinjan's architects replaced the polygonal choir area with the transept that characterizes the present edifice. They also facilitated access to the crypt by building two sets of stairs flanking the altar.

On Christmas Day of the year 1100 the church was the scene of the festive coronation of the Crusader king Baldwin I.

The Russian Abbot Daniel who visited the Church of the Nativity about that time (1106) describes it thus: "A large church in the form of a cross with a wooden roof rising above the Grotto of the Nativity. The roof is entirely covered with tin and the interior is ornamented with pictures in mosaic. It has 50 monolithic marble columns, and is paved with white slabs. There are three doors. Its length to the great altar is 50 *sagenes*, its width 20. Under the great altar is the Grotto of the Manger where Christ's Nativity took place, forming a fine and spacious cavern ...".

41

41. Remains of the wall mosaics.

42

42. The artistically-carved throne in the Greek Orthodox Church.

43

45

44

43. Icon of the Last Supper in the Greek
Orthodox Church.
44. Section of the iconostasis, the painted
screen separating the altar and the main
body of the church.
45. The Nativity depicted in a 13th-
century illuminated manuscript.

There are few places in the Holy Land more capable of arousing profound emotions within the pilgrim than the grotto in Bethlehem where, one silent, mysterious night some two thousand years ago, the events took place that changed the course of world history.

"Hic de Virgine Maria Jesus Christus natus est" — "Here Jesus Christ was born to the Virgin Mary", reads the inscription on the fourteen-pointed silver star embedded in the white marble on the spot where Jesus entered the world.

No one can ever forget this place after seeing it. It has inspired the most beautiful Christmas stories told in every language and has been represented in every possible manner — from great masterpieces in painting and sculpture to gaudy Christmas postcards printed in the thousands.

46. Father and daughter praying at the site of Jesus' birth.

46

47. Pilgrims at the Altar of the Nativity.

47

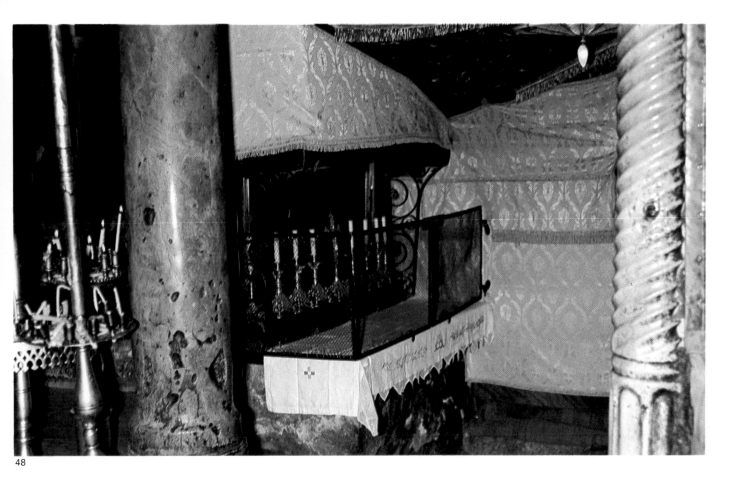

48

Another corner of the grotto, down three steps, opposite the Altar of the Nativity, contains the manger. Hewn out of the living rock, its sides were many years ago faced with marble. Stone troughs for feeding animals are quite common in this part of the world even today. The pilgrim, on contemplating the manger, will no doubt be reminded of the words the angel spoke to the shepherds: "And this shall be a sign unto you; ye shall find the babe wrapped in swaddling clothes, lying in a manger" (Luke 2:21).

"In this place heavenly love became manifest in our world. Hope was reborn and peace embraced the earth" (from an Oriental liturgy).

48. Altar of the three Magi facing the Manger.

49

49. Lamp in the Nativity grotto.
50. (overleaf) The famous silver star marking the place of Jesus' birth.

51

51. Bethlehem Christians assemble for the procession.
52. On Christmas Eve the peals of these church bells are broadcast around the world.

As each Christian church tends to cling to its own ancient traditions, it is not so surprising that many of the denominations represented in the Holy Land also follow their own religious calendar.

Western Catholics and Protestants celebrate the birth of the Saviour on the 25th of December. The Latin Patriarch is welcomed by the citizens of Bethlehem and conducted in festive procession to the Church of St. Catherine. The festivities include carolling by choirs from many countries. The bells ring out and the Christmas message is broadcast by radio throughout the Western world. The midnight celebrations reach their climax when, amid the rejoicing of the congregation, the Patriarch carries an image of the Christ child to the manger in the crypt below the Church of St. Catherine.

The Greek Orthodox and other Eastern Churches celebrate the Nativity thirteen days later, on the 7th of January, as they still follow the old Julian calendar. This colourful ceremony is celebrated in their festively-decorated Church of the Nativity.

The Armenian Christmas celebrations are held, according to an ancient Eastern tradition, on Epiphany, the 6th of January of the Gregorian calendar, which corresponds with the 19th of January of the Eastern calendar. Their Patriarch, too, is officially received in Bethlehem, and during the subsequent celebrations the much-tried Armenian people commemorate the apparition of God's Son at his birth, and his subsequent baptism in the River Jordan and his first miracle at Cana.

52

53

*53. The mayor of Bethlehem welcomes
the Latin Patriarch.*

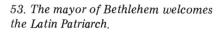

54

*54. Greek Orthodox bishops and priests
awaiting the start of the procession into
the church.*

55

*55. Welcoming the Armenian Church
hierarchy in Bethlehem.*

56

57

56. *The Roman Catholic Patriarch of Jerusalem carries the Christ child into St. Catherine's Church.*
57. *Armenian priests.*
58. *Midnight mass in the newly-restored St. Catherine's Church.*

59. *Stained-glass windows above the entrance of St. Catherine's Church.*

59

58

In A.D. 386 the Dalmatian priest Jerome arrived in the small town of Bethlehem from Rome. He secluded himself in a cave near the Grotto of the Nativity, to study the Bible and try to understand its deeper meanings. In Rome his strenuous activities as secretary to Pope Damasus had left him no time to pursue his scholastic ambitions. But even there a circle of female devotees had formed around him, who were equally eager to strengthen the foundations of their belief. One of these, a patrician lady called Paula, and her daughter Eustochium, followed Jerome to Bethlehem, where they founded a convent near the Cave of the Nativity.

Jerome, who had been taught Hebrew by a Jewish convert, began a translation of the Old Testament from the original Hebrew. The outcome, composing the main part of the famous Vulgate, would for the next 1,500 years form the official Bible of the Roman Catholic Church. Jerome also wrote numerous commentaries, which were eagerly discussed with Paula and Eustochium. The trio were utterly devoted to Bethlehem. Upon her arrival in Bethlehem Paula had said: "Yes, this will be my resting place; since the Redeemer himself has chosen this as his residence, this is where I too want to stay".

Her wish was fulfilled, and the graves of St. Paula and her daughter, as well as that of St. Jerome himself, can be found in the same crypt, close to the Grotto of the Nativity. They are reached via a staircase descending inside St. Catherine's Church.

60

60. Statue of St. Jerome in the atrium of St. Catherine's Church. Here he worked at his famous Bible translation, the Vulgate.

61/62. Partial views of vaulted arcades.

61

62

The Church of St. Catherine, also called *S. Catherina ad Praesepe* (St. Catherine's Church) was rebuilt and expanded by the Franciscans in 1888. In the course of the accompanying excavations, remains of Crusader buildings were discovered, which were incorporated into the new structure.

In 1852 Napoleon III, who considered himself successor to the French Crusader king Louis IX of France, canonized as St. Louis, had declared the entire church complex French property. This embroiled him with Russia, which espoused the rights of the Eastern Orthodox Churches; the resulting conflict became one of the causes of the Crimean War. Even after winning the war, Napoleon was still unable to enforce his claim to the Church of the Nativity as a whole; he succeeded, however, in the case of the adjoining Church of St. Catherine.

Only recently, in 1975, this church underwent another renovation with great attention to aesthetic detail. Several years earlier (1962-64) the Cave of St. Jerome and the adjacent Cave of the Innocent Children had been similarly restored. An archaeological survey undertaken during the restoration revealed that these caves, located a few metres to the north of the Grotto of the Nativity, were in pre-Byzantine days selected as a choice place for burial.

63. Entrance to the Cave of St. Jerome.

63

64

65

The Cave of the Innocent Children was named in memory of the children of Bethlehem who fell victim to Herod's paranoid fear and cruelty (Matthew 2:16). There is no suggestion, however, that these children were ever buried here; the proximity of Jesus' birthplace may be considered sufficient justification for a memorial at this site. The discovery during the excavations of traces of an entrance with a threshold confirms an earlier theory that these caves formed the original entrance to the Grotto of the Nativity and constituted the outer part of it.

The main altar in this impressive subterranean complex is devoted to St. Joseph. It was he who selected this "cave fashioned by the hand of God" for the birth of the Messiah. It was here that he is said to have had the dream which caused his fateful decision to flee to Egypt, in order to safeguard the child that had been entrusted in his care.

"And when they [the Magi] were departed, behold, the angel of the Lord appeareth to Joseph in a dream, saying, 'Arise and take the young child and his mother, and flee into Egypt, and be thou there until I bring thee word: for Herod will seek the young child to destroy him'. When he arose, he took the young child and his mother by night, and departed into Egypt: and was there until the death of Herod" (Matthew 2:13-15).

66

64. A modern iron-wrought grille in front of St. Paula's tomb.
65. Altar in the Cave of the Innocent Children.
66. The rock at the entrance to this cave is seen here; this is not the case at the Cave of the Nativity.
67. The Altar of St. Joseph.

67

68

68. *The Armenian beadle lighting a candle at the Grotto.*

69. *Greek pilgrims in Bethlehem.*

69

70. *European pilgrims leaving the Church of the Nativity by the south portal.*

70

Few biblical cities have exercised such a powerful attraction on the faithful as this small town in the Judaean Hills. Jews know it as the town where the matriarch Rachel is buried, and as the ancestral town of Ruth and David. Moslems associate it with the virgin Mariam and her son "Issa", who is considered one of their greatest prophets. But it is mainly Christians who for almost two thousand years have been congregating in Bethlehem in ever-growing numbers.

There exist ancient ties between Jerusalem and Bethlehem. Members of the family of Jesus were the spiritual shepherds of the primitive Judaeo-Christian community on Mount Zion in Jerusalem. Davidic enthusiasts thought that in them (Jesus, James,Simeon etc.) was fulfilled the prophecy of Micah: "And thou, Migdal Eder (Tower of the Flock), Ophil of the daughter of Zion, to thee shall it come, the former dominion shall come, the kingdom of the daughter of Jerusalem" (Micah 4:8). Hegesip (c. A.D. 150) and Epiphanios (c. 370) inform us that Jesus' brother James was given the honorary title of "Ophil", or "Oblias", since he was of the House of David. The other place in Micah's prophecy, the Tower of the Flock, was, according to Eusebius and Hieronymus (*Onomastikon*), situated a short distance east of Bethlehem, on the spot where the angel spoke to the shepherds while they were tending their flocks. There, long ago (see Genesis 35:21) Jacob had put up his tent and had allowed his flock to graze. It is typical of the Judaeo-Christian interpretation that Bible texts were applied to their own ideological and geographical situation.

71

72

72. The Christian Copts have their own grotto in Bethlehem: the Cave of the Innocent Children.

71. St. George and the dragon depicted in a relief on the outside wall of the Church of St. George.

An echo of those close links between Zion and Bethlehem sounds in the following lines, a greeting to Bethlehem, composed around the year A.D. 420 by the Jerusalem priest Hesichios:

FROM ZION I GREET THEE, BETHLEHEM
IN THE DAUGHTER I SEE THEE, THE MOTHER.

IN YOU A GUIDING STAR LIT UP,
AND IN THIS CITY A MULTITUDE OF FIERY TONGUES.

THE STAR GUIDED THE MAGI,
THE TONGUES ILLUMINATED PARTHIANS AND MEDES
AND ALL OTHER NATIONS WITH THEIR REDEEMING LIGHT.

THROUGH YOU THE BREAD WAS LEAVENED,
BUT ZION PREPARED THE MEAL.

YOUR MANGER NOURISHED THE LAMB,
BUT ZION LED IT TO THE ALTAR.

YOU WRAPPED JESUS IN SWADDLING CLOTHES,
BUT IN ZION HE BARED TO THOMAS HIS BREAST.

YOU SHELTERED THE VIRGIN WOMB
WHICH CONCEIVED, YET KNEW NO MAN,
BUT HERE IS A BRIDAL CHAMBER,
WHICH ADMITTED THE GROOM THROUGH LOCKED DOORS.

73. Greek Orthodox altar of Christ.

73

74. *The very names of the streets rekindle memorable events. On the way to the Milk Grotto one passes through this street with a sign written in English and in Arabic.*

The names of the streets in Bethlehem eloquently relate the story of the sites. To the east of Manger Square a narrow street leads to the Church of the Milk Grotto.

According to a 6th-century legend, the Holy Family sought refuge here during the Slaughter of the Innocents. Another version relates that St. Joseph, informed by an angel of the danger threatening the Child and the need to flee to Egypt, hastened Mary, who was nursing the Child. A few drops of milk fell on the ground and the rock turned from red to white. For many centuries Christians and Moslems have entertained a superstitious belief that the rock had acquired curative properties, and had power to aid lactation. It was customary for European pilgrims to chip off tiny pieces from the whitish rock and take them to the churches in their own towns. The earliest record of this practice is in the 7th century.

The façade of the church is a fine example of native workmanship, and the local artisans have shown their love and veneration of the site by building a staircase with a mother-of-pearl inlay. Inside the Grotto, in a cosy corner, we find a unique painting of the Virgin nursing the Child.

On the same street, is a Coptic church dedicated to the Holy Family's flight. In Egypt, almost every other Coptic church is dedicated to the Virgin and to events related to the Nativity and to the flight to Egypt. They are abundantly represented in Coptic and Ethiopian art.

75. *The vaulted entrance to the Virgin's Grotto.*
76. *The Nativity and the Flight to Egypt told in stone by local artists on the capitals of columns.*
77. *The influence of Italian art is clearly visible in this section of the façade of the Milk Grotto.*

THE ARMENIAN MONASTERY

To the south of the forecourt of the Church of the Nativity lies the fortress-like monastery of the Armenians. It incorporates a substantial nucleus of constructions dating from the Byzantine and Crusader periods. Within the monastery one can also find traces of Justinian's atrium. According to Armenian chronicles, the monastery in its present form antedates the Crusader epoch, which enables the visitor to visualize the dimensions of the original Church of the Nativity. The Armenian convent serves as a gigantic buttress to the southern part of the original entrance.

The Armenians are an ancient people with a rich culture. Originating in the plain of Mount Ararat, they adopted Christianity very early; Christianity was a state religion in Armenia as early as 301. Their bond with the Holy

78. Facing the arched entrance of the Armenian monastery is a well with a dedicatory inscription to which pious pilgrims attribute curative qualities.
79. The Armenian church steeple overlooking Manger Square.

80

80. A painting of Mary and Child hangs over the 17th-century gilt wood-carved altar in the church of the Armenian monastery.

81. These stairs lead to the Armenian monastery. Note the medieval masonry of the adjacent wall that has been preserved. 82. Near the baptismal font, an altar with an 18th-century painting depicting the Baptism of Christ.

Land goes back to early times. St. Jerome enumerates the Armenians among the nations visiting the Holy Land. There were major figures who came from distant Armenia in early desert monasticism, such as St. Euthymius. As well as simple folk and clergy, there were also princely visitors. Sixth-century Armenian mosaics have been found in Jerusalem, which have been identified as the vestiges of monasteries patronized by Armenian queens and kings. An elaborately-sculptured wooden panel at the entrance to the colonnaded nave of the Basilica of the Nativity is the only vestige of a royal visit by Armenian King Hethoum in 1227. The Armenian monastery, which now has six monks, was once a major centre for Armenian hermits. The most important period of monasticism was during the pontificate of the great ascetic Patriarch, Krikor Baronder, in the 17th century. Scribes here were active in the copying and illustration of Bibles.

On the walls of the rooms one may see the hundreds of graffiti left behind by countless pilgrims as mute reminders of their passage. One will also find *khatchkars* (stone lace slabs) inserted into the walls. In the arched vaults of the monastery one is shown a big colonnaded hall with Byzantine capitals, thought to be the lecture-hall of St. Jerome. Pilgrims give detailed accounts of St. Jerome's University. Quaresmius, in 1628, is particularly

informative; the same impressions are supplied by a later visitor, Nau, who saw the mentioned hall in 1683.

In the basement, one may observe the stable which housed the horses of the exhausted pilgrims who stayed overnight; and, in the corner, an obsolete olive-press with huge stones. There are underground water cisterns of great antiquity; a local tradition venerates one particular well, reputed to have curative qualities.

The monastery church is decorated with blue Armenian tiles and the three altars are sculptured in wood. It is famous for an old baptismal font, where many pilgrims vowed to have their children baptized. Overlooking Manger Square, the roof of the monastery offers a unique panoramic view of Bethlehem with its terraced environs. The monastery provides community services for Bethlehemite Armenians, who number about three hundred.

Within the complex of the Armenian monastery one can study the ancient methods of stone-dressing and trace a continuity of stone-laying traditions, such as early Byzantine walls alongside Justinian structures, or foundations of a Crusader tower with an early-Ottoman superstructure. In these intercommunicating halls and chambers one relives all these periods — not always tolerant of the other, but today mutually reinforcing each other.

83

83. A stone olive press dating back to the 15th century in the basement of the Armenian monastery.

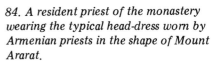

84. A resident priest of the monastery wearing the typical head-dress worn by Armenian priests in the shape of Mount Ararat.

85. It is believed that St. Jerome taught his disciples under the medieval high vaults of this colonnaded hall.

84

85

86

86. *Altar under the Syrian Orthodox church, made of the characteristic Bethlehem pink stone. It is a typical example of local workmanship.*

87. *The tower of the Greek Catholic church seen through the elaborate wrought-iron door.*

87

89

88. *The Carmelite church.*
89. *The Salesian church.*

88

Bethlehem is a heterogeneous town where one may find all persuasions of Oriental and Western Christianity represented.

There are Egyptian Copts with a chapel of their own, Armenians and Assyrians, with a modern church, a sizeable Greek Arab congregation and an equally large Catholic community. Through missionary and educational activities in the last century, Protestant churches began to have followers and converts, and today one finds many members of the Anglican and Lutheran churches. After his visit in 1898 Wilhelm II left a Lutheran church with Rhineland markings as a memento of his stay. The Uniate churches are also represented here. Prayers in Bethlehem may be said in all conceivable Eastern and Western tongues. It would be hard to enumerate all the chapels, large and small, in the town, but it seems that every shade of Christianity maintains institutions here in its own tongue. There is a continual mushrooming of educational institutions. If one scans Bethlehem's horizon, there is an unusual array of towers and belfries, domes and spires, houses of worship of all kinds, a legion, a unique parade of architectural forms, old and new, Oriental and Occidental — yet all harmonizing in one entity. There is no visible competition between these groups, each being satisfied with its foothold. There is an atmosphere of mutual tolerance and a pride of belonging to Bethlehem. When the bells of Bethlehem peal, one is invaded by the feeling that the human mosaic of Bethlehem is a triumph of a living and functioning ecumenic organism over sectarian dissent.

But above and beyond all, the Church of the Nativity exercises a mystical influence on the minds and souls of the residents of the town. It is their rallying-point and their source of inspiration. Within this edifice, Mankind's definitions of time, culture and religion give way to an overwhelming presence of God. The holy innocence of the Infant makes one see things in a different light: disagreements are forgotten; man is dwarfed by the Infant's message of love and peace. The Church of the Nativity unites all of Bethlehem. It has been the patron of their town; all their folklore has evolved around the Nativity. The imposing Church dominates the skyline of the town, challenging time and humanity, a symbol of the everlasting and the universal.

90

90. The dome of the Syrian Orthodox church. The minaret of the Mosque of Omar and St. Catherina's Church can be seen in the background.

91

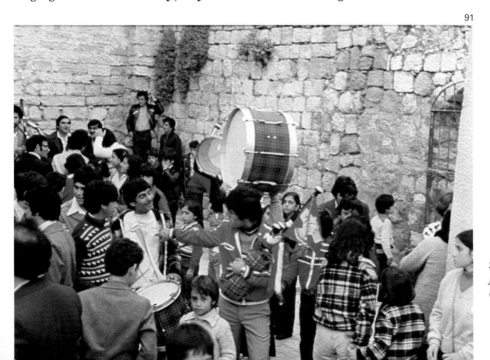

91. Bethlehem's band assembles before joining a Christmas procession to the Church of the Nativity.

92

92. *A sign-post indicates the direction and the distance to the Shepherds' Field and the Church of the Nativity.*
93. *A pastoral landscape that cannot fail to arouse biblical associations on the way to the Shepherds' Field.*

The Shepherds received the first tidings of the Nativity in a broad valley to the east of Bethlehem, where the townlet of Beit Sahur lies. This small town can be reached on foot from Bethlehem, and it has not altered much since the time of Boaz and Ruth. Villagers still raise corn and livestock and the landscape is dotted with herds of sheep and their young shepherds, grazing in the fertile fields and slopes. The precise location of the appearance of the angels to the shepherds is unknown, but of several sites venerated by Christians at different periods, the weight of tradition has centred on two, one is in the care of the Greek Church and the other is maintained by the Franciscans.

It is only natural that around an ancient holy place, others of lesser and later significance should be linked with different events in the same story. The value of such sites is not so much in their accuracy as in their teaching, and because they enable the pilgrim to remember and reconstruct the story in his mind. There are many traditions about the Shepherds' Field. One dates from the 7th century and, even earlier, Egeria refers to prayers held in the church of the Shepherds' Field. Another tradition points to the tombs of the three shepherds.

The new Greek church, which is still being completed, was erected near the traditional site of the Grotto of the Shepherds. For centuries, a monastery stood on the spot, but there is no mention of a grotto until the

94

95

*94-100. The shepherds of Bethlehem.
"And there were in the same country
shepherds abiding in the field, keeping
watch over their flock by night. And, lo,
the angel of the Lord came upon them,
and the glory of the Lord shone round
about them: and they were sore afraid.
And the angel said unto them, Fear not:
for behold, I bring you good tidings of
great joy, which shall be to all people.
For unto you is born this day in the city
of David a Saviour, which is Christ the
Lord ... The shepherds said to one
another, Let us now go even unto Bethlehem, and see this thing which is come
to pass, which the Lord hath made known
unto us" (Luke 2:8-15).*

96

101. A sign in Italian at the Shepherds' Field with the emblem of the Franciscan Order above it.

102. The new Greek Orthodox Church in the Shepherds' Field.

103. The cave traditionally believed to be the Grotto of the Shepherds under the Franciscan Church of the Angels.

Crusaders' time. The tradition of the site goes back to the year 670, and perhaps even to the time of the Roman Paula. The subterranean chapel, to which twenty-one steps descend, is venerated as the spot where an angel, surrounded by a supernatural light, appeared to the bewildered shepherds and sang "Glory to God in the highest: and on earth peace to men of good will". The grotto contains some paintings, and a few traces of Byzantine mosaic pavement.

Another site venerated by tradition is not far away. In travel literature it is known as *Siar al Ghanam* (Sheepfold). The site belongs to the Franciscans and was carefully excavated, revealing a vast monastic agricultural establishment, cisterns and grottoes.

According to evidence in the field, an early church dating from the 4th-5th century was enlarged in the 6th century, and stones from the octagonal construction of the Basilica of the Nativity were employed in the construction of its apse. The cave with an altar was traditionally looked upon as having been inhabited by the Shepherds.

Eusebius of Caesarea, bishop and scholar, writes that the Tower Eder, a thousand paces from Bethlehem, marked the place where the shepherds received the message. This was understood to be the "Migdal Eder" mentioned in the Bible (Genesis 35:21). St. Jerome was of the same opinion. The Calendar of Jerusalem (7th-8th century) indicates that to the east of Bethlehem was a monastery called *Poemnium* (of the flock), where the angel appeared to the shepherds. The Abbot Daniel — mentioned previously — calls the place *Agia Pimina* (holy pasture), and Peter the Deacon, in 1137, calls the church, which had a grotto with an altar, *Ad Pastores*. After the period of the Crusades, the church fell into ruin.

The present sanctuary, which was erected in 1953-54, stands on a large rock. It is built in the shape of a tent, a polygon with five straight and five projecting sides. The light which floods the interior reminds one of the strong light present when the angels announced the divine birth. Inside the church, the frontal and the upper part of the altar are decorated with fifteen panels depicting various scenes from the Annunciation to the arrival of the Holy Family in Egypt. On the door lintel there is a fine bronze relief. The church was designed by the celebrated architect, Barluzzi, and both the laying of the foundation stone and the dedication took place on Christmas Day. Nearby there are remains of a watch-tower, known as Eder Tower (Tower of the Flocks), which is now incorporated in the Franciscan Hospice.

Every year, at midnight on Christmas Day, these fields are crowded with thousands of pilgrims, singing Christmas carols to celebrate the joyous event.

Here, for the first time, was sung *Gloria in Excelsis:* "Glory to God in the highest, and on earth peace, good will toward men".

Just past the village is the fertile plain known as the Field of Ruth. Somewhere in this area took place the lyrical tale of Naomi and Ruth, gleaning in the barley fields of Bethlehem, which has left an indelible mark on the minds of countless generations. Ruth is unique in the history of womankind because her story is not primarily that of her love for a man, but of her devotion to her mother-in-law.

105

106

104

107

104/105. The tent-shaped Franciscan Church of the Angels in the Shepherds' Field. At this site was sung for the first time the hymn: "Glory to God in the highest, and on earth peace, good will toward men" (Luke 2:14).
106. A wall-painting above the altar in the church depicting the shepherds returning to their flocks after their visit to the Manger.
107. Archaeological finds near the church.

108

108. *The Greek Orthodox Church of St. Nicholas at Beit Jala has a square tower and glittering silver dome.*

109. *A general view of Beit Jala.*

110. *The Belfry of the Virgin of the Greek Orthodox Church at Beit Jala.*

110

BEIT JALA & BEIT SAHUR

There are two towns in close proximity to Bethlehem: Beit Jala and Beit Sahur, each with a population of about 8,000. Today, they seem like extensions of Bethlehem and there are no municipal boundaries dividing them. In the past these were villages of no consequence, but today one cannot overlook their economic and social significance.

The townlet of Beit Jala is located on a conspicuous hilltop, and has long been enjoyed as a summer resort. The greenery enhances the beauty of the landscape. Beit Jala is famous for the tasty apricot grown there — which is quickly snatched up when offered. There is a long tradition of weaving which today is using modern technological methods. The town also has a prosperous textile industry. The people of Beit Jala have distinctive brocaded costumes and, despite the invasion of modern ways and dress, they seem reluctant to abandon their age-old attire. The town is reputed for its master

109

stone-masons, and its sculptors have left their mark on many buildings and tombstones in Jerusalem and Bethlehem. Beit Jala people are renowned for being industrious and they possess a sharp acumen for trade.

There are four churches at Beit Jala, the most charming being the Greek Orthodox church of St. Nicholas, a Lutheran church and school and a German-run boarding school for girls, Talitha Qumi. The Latin Patriarchate Seminary, founded in Jerusalem in 1852, was transferred to Beit Jala the following year.

In the direction of Jerusalem is a curious shrine, probably of pagan origin, known as Badariya (*Badr* meaning "Full Moon"), which is venerated by Christians and Moslems alike. A string of factories extends into the orchards, and in recent years a lot of garage repair-work has been done in Beit Jala. Higher up in the town are several hotels where vacationers come to spend the hot summer months.

A road leads to Cremisan where the Salesian Fathers have a theological seminary, run a farm and produce a very fine wine which they sell. A short distance out of Beit Jala is the village of El Khadr with the Church of St. George, a popular site of pilgrimage.

Beit Sahur, to the north-east of Bethlehem, has a more pastoral setting. The olive groves dominate the horizon. It is not without folkloric interest to write a few lines about the olive-picking season, which extends over October and November. During the "season" the groves will be invaded by hundreds of villagers, male and female, young and old. In this crowd one will also find Bedouin women with their kohl-blackened eyes. Since antiquity, olives have been the main commodity for barter in these villages. The amount and quality of the crop is the topic of the day. It is an opportunity for gossip and social encounter and, at nighttime, the villagers gather around the olive press. The efficiency of mechanical methods has not left old stone presses idle. Olive oil flows for two months and is marketed to every town, churches receiving their share for lamps.

The origins of Beit Sahur go back to the Bronze Age. From its institutions and human composition it can be considered a sister town to Beit Jala. The Latin Patriarchate has a church with a very ornate altar and schools. A small church built in 1859 was completely transformed in 1951-52. The Sisters of the Rosary run the Girls' School. Just below it is the new church of the Greek Catholics, with a large school of 500 pupils run by the German Salvatorian Sisters. The Lutherans have a school too. It is a thriving town with many branches of industry, the best known being a plastics factory.

Beit Sahur like its counterpart has many beautiful villas, some with many stories. In 1880, a visitor wrote, "Nearly all the houses have now glass windows, a rare thing twenty years ago". Today, despite the town's modern aspect, it seems that it will never shake off its rural and romantic elements.

As one leaves the town one's eyes meet children carrying water from the well. One may wonder at the fact that the modern convenience of running water has not been able to prevail upon the age-old custom of storing water. The cisterns still have their devotees who assure their survival.

111

111. Sign in Greek and Arabic above the entrance to the Greek Orthodox church at Beit Sahur.
112. Courtyard of a church at Beit Sahur.
113. A shop securely closed by an old-fashioned door at Beit Sahur.
114. Villagers return home after shopping in town.

BETHLEHEM TODAY

No small amount of Jerusalem's celebrity can be attributed to the divine birth which took place in the Grotto of Bethlehem. Though the fluctuating fortunes of Bethlehem do not present the drama of Jerusalem, there exists a marriage of fate between the two towns — a bond shaped by history, by geographical proximity and by social and economic intercourse.

Situated 750 metres above sea-level, Bethlehem stands on two plateaus extending from east to west. It is surrounded by gorges and fertile terraces, and is bordered on the east and the south by the desert.

Archaeological evidence has shown that Bethlehem was inhabited in the Stone Age, from which time there has been a continuous evolution of human culture there. This insignificant town rose to prominence with the

115. A neon-lit street of Bethlehem at a short distance from Manger Square.

116

Nativity of the Lord. It attracted people from all walks of life — emperors, monks and common folk. Constantine, the Byzantine emperor, endowed it with an imposing church. In the Byzantine period it was a walled city with two towers, defended by the two deep gorges around it. It figures in the famous map of Madaba and in the accounts of such early pilgrims as Arculfus. The city sustained damages in the Samaritan revolt of 529, and Emperor Justinian (527-65) repaired its walls and embellished it. Tancred, at the head of one hundred horsemen, captured the city in 1099, fifteen days before Jerusalem fell to the Crusaders.

The new lords of Palestine decided to have their kings crowned in the Church of the Nativity. Baldwin I was the first to be so honoured, with great ceremony, in 1100. His coronation there was followed by that of Baldwin II, as a result of which Bethlehem came to enjoy royal favour. It was raised to the status of a bishopric, and Ascalon fell within its jurisdiction. The city was spared by Saladin and in the ensuing centuries, with the notable exception of its occupation by the Kharizmian Turks (1244), it led a peaceful existence. A wealth of travel literature exists, particularly about Jerusalem and Bethlehem, and from the 16th century, with the Ottoman Turkish rule of Palestine, information abounds concerning these two places.

116. The recently completed Bethlehem town hall.

117

118

119

117. The entrance to one of the many
old houses of Bethlehem.
118/119. Sunflower seeds are also bought
at the market-place.

121. A modern shop in Manger Square.

120. A craftsman skillfully carving a
mother-of-pearl object.

120

121

We have acquired a relatively accurate, statistical picture of the town from the Turkish land tax registers. The traveller, Affagart, found 50-60 households in 1533, and the population seems to have risen to 150 families when Doubdan visited the town in 1652. A century later 500 families were living in the town and Tobler mentions 3,300 inhabitants in 1845. A decade earlier Ibrahim Pasha had cruelly crushed a peasant revolt in Bethlehem and had razed the Moslem quarter of the town.

At the turn of the century, Bethlehem's population numbered 8,200 souls. By 1912 the population of Bethlehem had doubled as compared to the previous century, and had reached the record figure of 11,000. The number of inhabitants gradually diminished as a result of their forced conscription by the Turks in the Balkan War and the First World War. Epidemics also took their toll. The ebb of tourism was also a contributory cause for the mass flight of young people from Bethlehem. In 1922 the British found only 6,650 people living in the town; today, Bethlehem has a population of over 30,000.

Bethlehem is an Oriental town *par excellence*. One may encounter the unexpected at every corner. There are many houses of great age — the living testimony of past centuries. Rooftops mingle with domes, and the Crescent

123

124

122

125

122. Bethlehem schoolgirls going home.
123-125. Antique shops at the approach of the town.

126

126. Arched and grilled windows in the old section of Bethlehem.

is in constant communion with the Cross. Bethlehem is a market town, where you find people in various elaborate costumes. In the fruit and vegetable market, peasant women, some with hazel-green eyes, squat alongside Bedouin women, their eyes outlined with kohl. Plastic utensils may be bartered together with chickens, while the Bedouin women, with blue stars tattooed on their chins, will offer you hand-woven rugs.

As you wander away from the market-place you will run into the young folk who have altogether adopted new ways. Yet there is a strange feeling of continuity permeating this town. Traditions seem to be more enduring here, producing a curious coexistence of the ancient and the modern. As one admires an ultra-modern American limousine in one of the few motorable streets of the old section of the town, it is not unusual to see a young woman with a steeple head-dress (dating from the Middle Ages) emerging from some obscure archway. Only married women are entitled to wear this unique head-dress decked with coins, thus carrying their dowry on their head. The women of Bethlehem are renowned for their fine features, and travellers have invariably been struck both by their beauty and by their degree of emancipation. In former centuries it was not uncommon to find women working alongside the men in the mother-of-pearl workshops.

The streets are punctuated by the coffee-shops, the timeless forum of debate, and it is here that one can observe the respect that is still paid to age. The next stop must unquestionably be an Arab restaurant. The fragrance already fills the air. One can smell the herb-flavoured meat, the vine-leaves and the stupendous appetizers and, above all, the irresistible Arak: a beverage of grape-alcohol, flavoured with aniseed.

Bethlehem has a long tradition of producing master stone-masons. Every church in Jerusalem, in need of restoration, has availed itself of the skilled services of the Bethlehemite stone-dresser. As well as this reservoir

127. Bethlehem is built on the ridge of a hill and the streets slope up and down. Here, these peasant women ascend a steep street leading to the centre of the town.

127

of skilled craftsmen, there are quarries of high-quality Mezze and Malaki-
stones in the immediate vicinity of Bethlehem. Most of the houses in
Bethlehem are built of well-dressed and colourful pinkish stones. Iron
grilles are a decorative feature of the houses in Bethlehem, and one may
feast ones eyes on all the different combinations and variations of the
ironwork. The furniture inside some of these houses matches the beautifully-
carved façades. In almost every house one may find polygonal stools called
kursi, and table-tops inlaid with mother-of-pearl. Carved wooden beds
and cupboards enhance the beauty of the arched interiors. Bethlehemites are
famed for their hospitality, to the extent that one may feel overwhelmed
or even embarrassed by its warmth.

The large number of Mission Schools in Bethlehem is largely responsible
for the high level of literacy in the town. In earlier times pilgrims praised the
fluency of the inhabitants in foreign languages, and they have continued
to qualify themselves as excellent guides. Education has been a mixed
blessing for the town. Many of the educated youngsters, despairing of
finding professional fulfilment in their native town, have emigrated. Today,
there are sizeable *émigré* communities in South America, particularly in
Chile and Venezuela, some members of which have risen to high office in
these lands. Although this brain drain has had sad repercussions in the
demographic sense, it has allowed a flow of capital into Bethlehem. Today,
Bethlehem boasts an infrastructure of light industry which, thanks to the
efforts of its incumbent mayor Mr. Elias Freij, is transforming the face of
the town. Bethlehemites have always been an enterprising people who have
dared to brave the seas and travel to remote lands; in centuries past they
have travelled as far as Australia, the Far East and Europe. They are also
reputed for their artistry and sophisticated level of craftsmanship in olive-
wood and mother-of-pearl. The town has long been surrounded by vast

128

128. An old woman looks out of a grilled window with a carved-stone lintel.

129. A peaceful garden on the outskirts of the town.

129

130/131. Grilles, arches and pink stone are the main features of the old houses. 132. Out of the shadows of the dark archway, emerges into the bright sunshine a young couple carrying a cradle.

groves of olive trees, and wood-carving in Bethlehem is older than record. Although nowadays we are witnessing an ebb in artistry and the mechanization of many ancient skills, a lot of the workshops still produce religious objects using charmingly primitive, quasi-biblical methods.

Bethlehem owes its prosperity to the Church of the Nativity, and local industry in the past has focused on religious objects. We read in pilgrim reports about models of the Holy Sepulchre and the Grotto of the Nativity, carved in wood or in stone, being offered to the visitors. Some objects were made of semi-hard stone brought from Nebi Musa, near the Dead Sea.

Mother-of-pearl is the main industry and the pride of Bethlehem. In earlier times the raw material was brought by caravans from the Red Sea. Later on, one finds evidence of Bethlehemite traders purchasing this semi-precious material in New Zealand and Australia. The variety of its use is boundless; it is to be found in book-bindings, in furniture and jewelry, and decorative objects. Bethlehem has adopted mother-of-pearl as its trade mark, developing special methods for its use.

There is a high concentration of institutions in the northern part of the city, their number being out of proportion to the size and cultural significance of the town. In the last century, one finds a mushrooming of foreign institutions. The town attracted missionaries, religious orders, volunteers and people motivated by Christian charity. The services offered by some of these institutions go beyond the confines of Bethlehem. Many have benefited from the specialized education offered, and others have availed themselves of the medical and welfare services.

French and Italian Catholic institutions were the pioneers, followed by Protestant societies of other nations. There are orphanages, homes for the aged and vocational training schools. The Italian Salesians, who came in 1863, have rendered invaluable service in training generations of skilled

133

134

135

136

133. Time has sculptured the trunk of this ancient olive tree into intricate patterns.

134. The mass-produced olive wood religious objects still require the finishing touch of this young artist before they are shipped to many parts of the world.

135. A wood-carved partition panel on display at one of the shops.

136. A Bethlehem artist carving olive wood.

137

137. Students at the Bethlehem university library.

professionals. Their technical school, with its many branches, has become the pride of Bethlehem. The French have established the best network of schools and medical services. Today, Bethlehem has become a university town. Since its inception, the new campus has become a centre of cultural activity. Some of its research is oriented towards rural development. The American Christian Mission has a hospital for crippled children, and the orthopaedic care given there is of expert quality.

No less important work is being done by the Caritas Children's Hospital run by the Sisters of the Holy Cross of Metzingen founded in 1884. Quite recently this fine Swiss-German institution inaugurated an ultra-modern hospital. The Swedes are to be commended for their twin institutions for retarded children, one in Jerusalem and the other in Bethlehem.

Admirable work has been going on in the German-run S.O.S. children's village. It takes in abandoned children and orphans and organizes them into family units. After many years of work it can be considered a successful experiment in underprivileged child-care. The Arab Women's Society is doing indispensable work in the cultural and welfare spheres.

Tribute has to be paid to the Sisters of Dorothea, for their institute for the deaf and blind, and to the British Bible Land Society which has its own home for the blind. There is a score of institutions, hospitals and maternity wards run by all types of religious orders. The Rosary, the White and St. Joseph Sisters carry out their charitable and educational functions in humility and

138

138. Time for play at S.O.S., the children's village.

anonymity, and the list is endless. Special mention should be made of the Franciscan Order, which was the first Catholic order to establish itself in Bethlehem. It has played a central role in the development of the town since the Middle Ages. Besides its educational and economic contributions, it is considered to be responsible for the introduction of the art of mother-of-pearl into Bethlehem.

On the fringes of Bethlehem, dominating the northern approach of the town, stands Tantur, the Ecumenical Institute for Advanced Theological Studies. Here in 1876, the Hospice of the Order of Malta was opened, and the chapel was built in the same year. When Pope Paul VI visited the Holy Land in 1964, he asked Father Hesburgh, President of Notre Dame, to organize an institute that would become an ecumenical study centre. Its mission is being faithfully fulfilled and holds great promise for the promotion of brotherly understanding between the Churches. The institute has served and housed clergy from all five continents. One of its primary objectives has been to establish contact with the Oriental Churches, and there are indications that these contacts have been mutually beneficial and fruitful. The huge library of the institute, wonderfully organized by the Benedictine Fathers of Montserrat (Spain), serves the academic public.

Despite its outwardly modern aspect, Bethlehem has lost little of its aura of biblical and medieval romance. It is a town touched by holiness yet pulsating with modern life.

The Holy Land has not been blessed by abundant water resources, and the problem has been compounded by scanty rainfall. Since biblical times, the water sources and wells have been the sites of many great events. Jacob's and Rogel's Wells and Mary's Well are some of the better known. There is almost a water cult, and many cisterns have become sanctified and have had miracles attributed to them: they heal sick bodies and souls, and cast out demons. In this part of the world, for thousands of years, the chisel of man has constantly been at work hewing the rock in search of water. Many a town has fallen in the Holy Land for lack of water resources. Water has been a strategic asset; in every siege the defenders had two overriding concerns: fortifications and water. There were cisterns of all shapes and sizes: some served as abodes for hermits, others have the appearance of natural gaping quarries. A lot of the songs, poetry and folklore of this land revolve around water, and many a dispute has arisen about water rights. Since antiquity rulers in the Holy Land have been obsessed by the

139

140

139. Approach to Solomon's Pools.
140. One of the three pools.

141. The entrance to a 17th-century caravanserai near Solomon's Pools.

141

problem of drought and have developed elaborate systems of water storage. In this, the Roman methods are unsurpassed. The pools of Solomon bear testimony to their thoroughgoing knowledge of the construction of water reservoirs and aqueducts. The prime concern since the First Temple period has always been to maintain Jerusalem's supply of water. About five kilometres south of Bethlehem, situated in a small valley, lie three huge rectangular reservoirs of fabulous size. The pools are unquestionably of great antiquity. There is little ground for attributing the pools to Solomon, and it was probably Pontius Pilate (Procurator of Judaea, 26-36) who conceived the idea. The three pools, constructed on levels, partly hewn in rock and partly enclosed in masonry, with flying buttresses, were constructed with a view to the water being carried to a distance; the water flowed as far as Jerusalem by force of gravity. Even today, considerable portions of its route between Bethlehem and Jerusalem are still strewn with terracotta piping, and this very same conduit system, many times repaired, was in use until 1947. The average size of the pools is 150 metres by 70 metres, and between 7 and 15 metres deep. Their combined volume is about 160,000 cubic metres, which was a very large amount in the days when they were built. The lowest of the three is always the first to be filled, followed by the two others in succession, and they empty in the same order.

In 1904, during construction work near the Tomb of Rachel, a high-level aqueduct came to light, which was ascribed to the time of Septimus Severus (195). Roman inscriptions on the stones found mention certain centurions of the Roman Tenth Legion. In the vicinity there is also an older aqueduct attributed to the time of Pilate.

Continuing along the pools we reach the small picturesque village of Artas, whose name derives from the Latin *hortus* (garden). Below the village lies the monastery of Hortus Conclusus.

142. King David's Wells.
143. Part of the Roman aqueduct near Rachel's Tomb.

142   143

144. *View of Beit Sahur with Herodium on the horizon.*

144

145

145. *The entrance to the fortified palace built by King Herod the Great on top of a conical hill at Herodium.*

To the south-east of Bethlehem a cone-shaped hill rises out of the ground. This was King Herod's summer palace retreat. Josephus the historian describes it as "an artificial rounded hill in the form of a woman's breast". It is also known as the Mountain of the Franks.

According to Josephus, who is the only literary source, King Herod wished to be buried in Herodium, and his body was borne 39 kilometres from Jericho for interment here.

It is assumed that the site was destroyed by the Romans in A.D. 70, and that Bar Kokhba took advantage of its strategic position in his revolt against the Romans.

The hunt for Herod's tomb has not yielded much as yet. A fortress with four towers has come to light, in addition to Roman baths. In recent years three Byzantine churches with rich decorative mosaic floors have also been uncovered in the Lower Herodium area.

From the summit, a panorama of singular beauty spreads before your eyes.

146. *Remains of columns inside the stronghold which Herod intended to use as a refuge for himself and his family in the event of trouble in Judaea.*

146

MAR ELIAS

Midway between Jerusalem and Bethlehem, pleasantly situated on the saddle of a hill, stands the Greek monastery of Mar Elias. On reaching its gates, the traveller is confronted by a panoramic view of Bethlehem and Herodium.

Tradition holds that the prophet Elijah slept here on his flight from Queen Jezebel's wrath. Another version claims that a Greek bishop of Bethlehem, called Elias, was buried here in 1345. The most plausible version is that the sepulchre of St. Elias, a 5th-century Patriarch of Jerusalem, lies here. Originally, Elias was a monk of Nitria in Egypt. After the Council of Chalcedon, rifts appeared among the thousands of monks who peopled the hundreds of monasteries in the Egyptian desert. Elias, in painful despair over this split of the Universal church, took the route to Palestine in 457. He came to consult St. Euthymius, whose monastery was situated between Jerusalem and Jericho, and was a centre for many novices like Saba and Theodoros who wished to be initiated into the rigours and discipline of the desert. Elias decided to establish his monastery on the fringe of the Judaean Desert.

Three different types of monasteries then existed: in the city, in the desert and in the agricultural plain. The last type cultivated such crops as olives and grapes, and represented a distinctly new departure from the monastic ideal, in which the superiority of labour is upheld. Mar Elias belonged to this last category.

147

147. Christ Pantocrator painted on the dome of the recently rebuilt church of Mar Elias Monastery.

148. The Monastery of Mar Elias built in the 11th century.

148

149

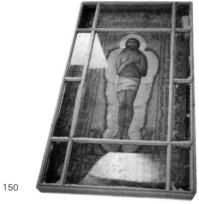

150

149. The bell-tower and silver dome of the Monastery of Mar Elias.
150. A tapestry depicting Jesus.
151. The Ecumenical Institute for Advanced Theological Studies.

152. Adjacent to the Monastery of Mar Elias, this ornate bench bears engraved inscriptions in several languages.

152

151

Elias' reputation won him the Patriarchal Seat of Jerusalem in 494, and during the rest of his career he waged a relentless war against the defenders of Monophysitism.

The actual monastery seems to have been erected at an unknown date by a Bishop Elias, whose tomb could be seen in the monastery church up to the 17th century. The monastery was rebuilt in the Crusader period. It has belonged to the Georgians, who possessed other monasteries like the Holy Cross Monastery in Jerusalem. Exorbitant taxation forced them out of the holy places in the Ottoman period.

Many miracles are attributed to Mar Elias. It is a popular site for pilgrims, and today we can still witness a colourful annual pilgrimage. To this day, as in the past, many children are vowed to Mar Elias. The saint is thought to respond to the requests of barren women and ailing children.

Many crosses are cut into the walls of the church — memorials of unknown pilgrims. The monastery is popularly considered to be a protector on the roads.

To this day, on Christmas Day, the Patriarchs pause here before making their solemn entry to Bethlehem. The Patriarch is received at Mar Elias by the notables of the area. From Mar Elias, the pace of the motorcade is set by horses, a custom which has been continued to the present day.

Near Mar Elias opposite Tantur, there is a vast field covered with innumerable small pebbles, which has always struck the imagination of the local residents, and has furnished a subject for one of those moral stories with which the East abound: "One day, a man was sowing chick-peas in that field," tells a pious legend, "when Mary (others say Jesus), passing by, asked him: 'What are you sowing there, my friend?'' 'Stones', was the answer 'Very well, you will reap stones'. And truly, when the sower came to gather them, he found nothing but petrified peas". From that time the Field of Grey Peas has reminded passers-by of the punishment that follows a lie.

THE DESERT MONASTERIES

The centre of Christian monasticism had shifted from Egypt to the Holy Land during the latter half of the 5th century. The forbidding wastes of the Judaean Desert offered an ideal setting for these ascetics who came mainly from Cappadocia, Asia Minor and Armenia in quest of perfection and solitude. The desert was considered a nursery of the souls. John the Baptist had preached in the wilderness. Jesus had returned to the desert, and so had Paul.

The most prominent monastic centres of these austere times lie to the east of Bethlehem. As one drives into the Judaean wilderness, passing the fertile olive orchards, one is gradually ushered into a new landscape, half desert, marked with occasional patches of cultivation; a succession of rounded, rocky and trackless hills. It was in this parched waste land that anchorites were initiated into the ways of the desert.

They chose to live at the limits of human nature. Unremitting in their fasts, and even drinking water sparingly, they competed with each other for feats of endurance. Yet these ascetics, leading a life of extreme self-denial, were active scholars and were responsible for the spiritual revival of the period. Most of the early hagiographic literature about the lives of the saints and stories of martyrs were recorded here. These monastic settlements played a leading role in the development of the liturgy and dogma. The monks of the desert were innovative, and in many respects they broke new ground.

Although they led a contemplative existence in their cells, work was nevertheless an integral part of their life. There was a highly-organized system of labour — a rule binding on the abbot no less than on the monks. Thus monasticism evolved in the desert, becoming the institution from which Western monasticism took its roots, and providing an important source for Christian inspiration throughout the centuries.

The largest and most highly-organized of these monasteries is that of

153

153/154. Views of the Monastery and Church of St. Theodosius "Where the Three Wise Men from the east rested after paying homage to Jesus in Bethlehem".

155

St. Theodosius. Born in Cappadocia in 432, he came to Jerusalem as a youth. He retired to the Church of Kathisma, and one day was divinely directed to a cave where, according to tradition, the wise men had stayed the night they left Bethlehem (Matthew 2:12). It was here that he founded the monastery which was to become the most populous, at one time housing 693 monks. It contained four churches, and services were held

156

155. The Church of St. Theodosius was recently rebuilt, incorporating remnants of the old Crusader building into the new construction.
156. One of the Greek monks of the monastery by the dome of the burial vault of St. Theodosius.
157/158. The burial cave of St. Theodosius.

157

158

in four languages: Greek, Georgian, Armenian and Slavic. The monastery was fortified and a visitor in 1185 saw many towers. Not all the monks lived in the monasteries, however. Many dwelt in cells; these "cells" were inaccessible caves reached only by ladders. Some led a life of silence and contemplation; they lived out of sight or sound of each other. Others were preoccupied in the intensive study of the Scriptures, and Saturday nights the cell-dwellers would come into the monastery for Sunday Liturgy and the common meal.

If one reads the works of Cyril Scythopolis, the historian of the lives of the saints, one is struck by the international character of Judaean monasticism. Here, people of all races and creeds prayed and worked together; a living testimony to the Universal Church. Here common folk mingled with bishops of the Church, who came to these barren valleys to escape their fame. They went off to the desert not to escape temptation but to invite it.

Today, after fifteen centuries of unbroken history, the monastery still lives on. Eighteen steps bring you down to the cave where the founder, St.

Theodosius, rests in peace. He died at the great age of 105. In a cave recess
a cluster of skulls of anonymous monks can be seen, with crosses between
their eye-sockets. The present Church of St. Theodosius, which was completed in 1952, stands on the ruins of a clover-shaped Byzantine church.

The road to the monastery of Mar Saba is bumpy but negotiable. There
is nothing to relieve the monotony, except the occasional herds of goats,
and while driving in this utter wilderness one has the irresistible feeling
of stepping out of time. Suddenly the monastery of Mar Saba, with its
girdle of walls and towers, comes into view. It is a unique structure, built
in a highly individual way. A raging torrent would not disturb the absolute
tranquillity; here is a stronghold of peace. After a moment's reflection, one
remembers that it was to this remote gorge that the centre of the whole
desert movement moved. The monastery is a jewel in the cave-riddled
canyon. The scene is so singularly wild, that verbal description can give
little or no idea of it.

The monastery of Mar Saba is immense. It has 110 rooms and ten
monks still dwell within its walls, spending their time in meditation and
work. The founder, St. Saba, came from Cappadocia in the 5th century.
Originally he had settled in the Wadi al-Nar (the Wadi of Fire). Tradition
lays claim to supernatural beginnings, and one is still shown the rock-cut
sanctuary to which the saint was divinely directed. St. Saba, who lived to
be 94, exerted great influence on the emperors of his time, including
Justinian, and the monastery enjoyed imperial patronage during this forma-
tive period of monasticism. He became the champion of the Chalcedonians
around which controversies raged at his time. He also had to deal with other
heresies. The numerous anchorites, while being men of great virtue, were
also very independent of mind and this often led to lack of discipline and
heresies. Many came to seek counsel and spiritual guidance, and they
included Empress Eudoxia.

The monastery, which acquired great renown, housed five thousand
monks in its heyday. In the centre of a paved courtyard, in an octagonal
domed chapel, lay the bones of St. Saba. His relics were carried off to
Venice in 1256 but recently, upon the request of Pope Paul VI, the bones
were restored to their first resting place. Today, the saint's body rests
under an elaborately-sculptured canopy in the monastery church.

159

159. View of Herodium taken from the belfry of the Church of the Nativity.

The chief memorial to the saint is his grotto, shown on the southern side
of the monastery, near the guest chamber. A passage in the rock leads to
the grotto adjoining which is a smaller chamber called the Lion's Grotto.
One day, as legend has it, the saint entered his cave and found it occupied
by a lion. St. Saba fearlessly said his prayers and fell asleep. The lion
dragged him out of the cave twice, but the saint, objecting to these proceed-
ings, assigned a corner of the grotto to the lion, whereupon they live
peacefully together thereafter.

In a rock fissure nearby is a palm tree, reputed to have been planted by
St. Saba. The dates which it bears, say the monks, have no pits.

Since its foundation women have never been allowed to enter the
monastery. Opposite Mar Saba stands a two-storeyed tower with an oratory
dedicated to Simon the Stylite. From the so-called Women's Tower, which

160

160. *The dwellings of the monks of Mar Saba Monastery.*

is also known as the Tower of Eudoxia, one has a superb view of the *lavra* and of the gorge 180 metres below. The canyon, which is a succession of precipices, is dotted with "cells" and cave sepulchres. The most elaborate cave is that of St. John Silentiarius which has several levels and openings. One of the most striking caves is that of Arcadios.

There is a long tradition of hospitality to strangers. The *lavras* professing a high degree of austerity were open to strangers. They had hospices for guests in the towns, while the monasteries had their counterparts in the towns, known as *metochions*. A small *metochion* after the name of St. Saba was situated near David's Tower, where the famous 12th-century traveller Abbot Daniel lodged. Mar Saba who died in 533, had founded three other *lavras* and six monasteries, besides four hospices. Almost a century later, the Persians were to find as many as 137 monasteries throughout the Holy Land.

In the incense-laden light of the monastery, one is overwhelmed by the host of icons — iconoclasm never penetrated these walls. Hundreds of icons cover the high walls, but the richness of the painting never over-

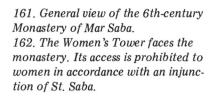

161. *General view of the 6th-century Monastery of Mar Saba.*
162. *The Women's Tower faces the monastery. Its access is prohibited to women in accordance with an injunction of St. Saba.*

162   161

163

163. An icon depicting the burial of St. John of Damascus.

comes the austerity of its theme. An unusual parade, a unique grouping of figures: militant and ascetic saints, clothed only in their own hair. The icons are like a window through which the divine is looking out. Some are strongly didactic, others have a narrative and documentary quality. One of the outstanding paintings is a representation of the Day of Judgement. The Deity is enthroned among angels and the spirits of good men. Beneath is a gigantic figure weighing the souls as they ascend. On one side, an equally gigantic "minister of punishment" stands in the midst of flames. On the other, Elias is fighting Antichrist; and in the background, the graves are giving up their dead.

Some of these icons have become legendary for their miracles. They weep, fly, are handed down from heaven, washed up on the tides, they induce rain, effect cures, cast out demons, ease pain, they will return lost children and animals, and strike men dumb and blind. They are a living record of fifteen hundred years of ascetic and artistic production — a labour of faith and love. A visit to the monastery may be concluded by a visit to the tomb of St. John of Damascus, the mighty defender of orthodoxy; he was to be known for his theological polemic and mystic treatises. Born in Damascus, St. John was a Greek theologian and Doctor of the Church. He abandoned public life in 716 and became a monk at the monastery of St. Saba where he wrote a treatise in defence of icon worship. His most famous work was a treatise dealing with Orthodox faith.

In the same chamber one finds scores of skulls of monks who suffered martyrdom at the hands of the Persians in 614.

As one drives back to the Grotto of the Nativity, where most of these ascetics took their oath, one labours under the feeling that these austere monks truly were the "sentries who keep watch on the walls of the city".

164

164. This edifice marks the site where St. Saba was originally buried. His remains were transferred to Venice by the Crusaders and have recently been brought back to Mar Saba. The saint is now buried in the monastery chapel.

BETHLEHEM

TO JERUSALEM
8 Km.

To Rachel's Tomb

To Rachel's Tomb

MORADEH STREET

CHILDREN STREET

HEBRON ROAD

(DHEISHEN STREET)

Protestant Cemetery

TO CREMISAN
TO FIELD SCHOOL
TO BEIT IALA
2 Km.

TO EZION BLOCK
TO BEER SHEVA
TO HEBRON 28 Km.

MAKFUFFEN ST.

MANGER STREET

MANGER STREET

S.O.S. Children's Village

Monastery of the Christian Brothers

(Freres Convent)

The Holy Land Christian Mission

ORIENT STAR ST.

STAR STREET

KING DAVID ST.

PAUL VI STREET

AMAL STREET

CHILDREN STREET

FRERES STREET

WARDIYEH ST.

St. Joseph's Church

French Hospital Church of the Holy Family

Cheshire Home

(St. Joseph's Sisters Convent)

King David's Wells

Catholic Action Club

MANGER STREET

Bethlehem Cinema

Women's Union Club

Nunnery of the Sisters of St. Joseph

BSELEH ST.

PAUL VI STREET

EL BATIN STREET

RAJUL ST.

Handal's Hotel

MIDAN STREET

FRERES STREET

SALESIAN ST.

STAR STREET

FARATMEI ST.

STREET

KII'A STREET

BASSA STREET

Salesian Convent

Church

Post Office

WAD MA'ALI STREET

WAD MA'ALI ST.

Greek Catholic Convent

Terra Sancta Convent

STAR STREET

TO BEIT SAHUR 1 Km.
TO SHEPHERDS' FIELD 3 Km.
HERODION 9 Km.

BEIT SAHUR ST.

BEIT SAHUR ST.

SHEPHERDS ST.

ATAN STREET

CARMEL STREET

Lutheran Christmas Church

FARATTEN STREET

FAKKOREH

PAUL VI STREET

STAR STREET

MANGER STREET

Terra Sancta College

SAFF STREET

Syrian Orthodox Church

Old Bethlehem Home

Police Department

Palace Hotel

Latin Convent

Greek Orthodox Convent

Carmelite Convent

KANAH STREET

Market

Omar Mosque

Manger Square

New Commercial Centre

Basilica of the Nativity

Armenian Convent

Carmelite Nunnery

Municipality

Tourist Information Office

MILK GROTTO ST.

ANATREH STREET

Coptic Orthodox Church

Chapel of the Milk Grotto

Franciscan Convent

KANAH STREET

JUBAI'A STREET

HINDAZEH STREET

ATAN STREET

ANATREH STREET

0   50   100   150 Meters

0   50   100   150 Yards

SAFF STREET

ADDITIONAL PHOTOGRAPHY

Photo Garo Nos. 12, 13, 18, 27, 28, 29, 45, 53, 55, 56, 57, 115, 120, 121, 122, 132, 136, 137, 138, 151, 161; David Harris No. 4; Israel Department of Antiquities and Museums No. 25; Municipality of Bethlehem No. 116; Father Bargil Pixner No. 8; Zev Radovan Nos. 21, 54.

Map p. 76: Carta Jerusalem.